S0-BFC-543

SUMMARY OF

CATCH
AND
KILL

LIES, SPIES, AND A CONSPIRACY TO PROTECT PREDATORS

BY
RONAN FARROW

PROUDLY BROUGHT TO YOU BY
ANTHONY KING

ISBN: 978-1-950284-55-9

Anthony King

Copyright (c) 2019

All rights reserved. No part of this publication may be reproduced, distributed, or transmitted in any form or by any means, including photocopying, recording, or other electronic or mechanical methods, without the prior written permission of the publisher, except in the case of brief quotations embodied in critical reviews and certain other noncommercial uses permitted by copyright law.

Disclaimer

This book is a summary and meant to be a great companionship to the original book or to simply help you get the gist of the original book.

Table of Contents

EXECUTIVE SUMMARY

Ronan Farrow's **Catch and Kill** is an extraordinary piece which beautifully and powerfully captures the story of his quest to expose Weinstein's distasteful activities to the world. It goes beyond mere storytelling, into taking the reader long on a deep journey of his day to day struggles to get the story out. This book will restore clarity to you, as well as stir up a seventh sense within you that will seek to look out for misdemeanors and find ways to address these ills.

CHAPTER 1: TAPE

KEY TAKEAWAYS

- McHugh was a big gun in the TV world
- McHugh was one of the smartest editors I have ever met

Finding out it was not going to air, I was livid. What on earth did that mean? My producer had just called to say that a series of investigative reports which we had both been working on was not going to air the next day, and that we had to move it forward. At a time like this, rescheduling wasn't even what I needed, or wanted to hear. Nevertheless, I pressed on to find out when it was being rescheduled to, but all I got was a response saying he'd call me back. I mean, for real?

My producer, McHugh was a big gun in the TV world-having worked at Fox and MSNBC, and Good Morning America. When I was assigned to work with him, my boss who put us together remarked that he spoke like a farmer, and that we both made no sense being together. Wondering why I was being paired with this person, my boss simply said that we would be good for one another. Huh! I began working with him anyway, even though he was unconvinced at first. I, for one, did not have my life hidden from public glare. My mom was an actress, and my father was a director. At some point in my childhood, my father was accused by my younger sister of sexual harassment, following which he went after another of my sisters, and eventually married her. Determined to make a name for myself amidst this craziness, I went off to college and took up a deal, where I anchored a midday show on MSNBC; a deal which would last four years. Initially, the show started badly, but later went on to have good reviews. Little did people notice that the show had been cancelled, for on so many occasions, people would walk up to me, saying they loved the show and watched it on a daily basis. I'd respond by telling them it was really nice to say that.

At this time, I had moved over to network, where I was working as an investigative correspondent. My producer, McHugh thought of me as a young, famous girl who was looking for a means to get occupied, merely because my contract lasted far longer than my TV show did. And I guess we both came to a consensus here, although the bottom-line for me was for everyone to like me.

Because I was working directly with a producer, I had no choice but to embark on long flights and trips with him. Initially, I used to do a lot of talking to fill up for the silence growing between us. Soon after however, our working together began to take a positive turn. My investigative series and nightly news had bought us both some mutual level of respect. And yeah, I must give this to him- my producer, McHugh was one of the smartest editors I have ever met. And together, we loved working tough!

CHAPTER 2: BITE

KEY TAKEAWAYS

- Harvey Weinstein abandoned college to start up a business with his brother and his friend.
- Weinstein was well known for was his bullying, threatening manner of doing business

Ever since the first studios were established, a few movie executives were as overriding and overbearing as Harvey Weinstein. Weinstein cofounded the production-and-distribution companies Miramax and the Weinstein Company, where he assisted in the re-invention of certain movies. At the Oscars, his movies had received nothing less than three hundred nominations. The same was the vase with any other ranking as he continually led the award ceremonies.

Weinstein abandoned college to start up a business with his brother and his friend, Bob and Burger. This business of theirs specialized in concert promotion. Later however, Weinstein began screening the films he eventually came to fall in love with. Establishing Miramax, an outfit named after their parents- Miriam and Max, himself and Bob began collecting small foreign films. Weinstein was able to turn these films into events, receiving multiple awards.

Disney came into the picture in the early nineties, acquiring Miramax. In the 200s, when things fell out between the brothers and Disney, they founded a new firm- The Weinstein company. Within a very short period of time, they were able to raise good money in funding. At this time, Weinstein had not recovered his good old days, but he successfully won back-to-back Best Picture Oscars for The King's Speech in 2010 and The Artist in 2011. At some point in time, he got married, had a divorce and later went on to marry an ambitious actress whom he had been casting in small roles.

One thing Weinstein was well known for was his bullying, threatening manner of doing business. He was scary, and would face rivals square-faced, eye-to-eye. For him, the months that led to the 2016 presidential election were just like any other, with noting spectacular about them. He was at a cocktail party for William J. Bratton, the former New York City police commissioner, enjoying the moment with Jay Z and strengthening his ties with the Democrats.

All through the year, Weinstein had been a major part of the Hilary Clinton campaign, pushing messages and emails around to get people to vote for her. When the year came to an end, Weinstein had successfully raised good dollars, in hundreds of thousands for Clinton. Some days later, Weinstein was at the St. James Theatre, attending another fundraiser for Clinton, of which he was part of its production. This fundraiser alone produced an additional two million dollars towards her campaign. And while Weinstein was no longer the center of attraction like he was back in the days, he was still able to wield a considerable amount of influence within the elite sphere. Just about that time, Weinstein mailed his lawyers, David Boies inclusive, about the Black Cube Group from Israel contacting him through Ehud Barak. Now, Barak was the former prime minister of Israel and chief of the General Staff of the Israeli military, and the firm he mentioned to Weinstein was a strategist firm with branches all over the world. Later that month, Boies's company and the Black cube went into a confidential agreement, with Boies's colleagues wiring a hundred thousand U.S. dollars for the first phase of the job. In all of the documents that concerned the assignment, Weinstein's identity was often concealed, as he was constantly referred to as "the end client" or "Mr. X."

CHAPTER 3: DIRT

KEY TAKEAWAYS

- Sometime in June 2016, Howard had gathered a bunch of dirt about Trump
- On a routine basis, the AMI blackmailed its employees, by withholding the publication of damaging information in exchange for tips.

Just before the elections finally hit home, sometime in the first week of November 2016, a rather unusual message was sent forth by Dylan Howard- the editor in chief of the National Enquirer. Howard instructed an employee to et everything out of the safe and shred all the documents in there. On that particular day, he seemed to be panicky. Just before he gave the instruction, the Wall Street Journal had placed a call across to the Enquirer requesting for comments regarding a story that concerned both Howard and David Pecker- the CEO of the Enquirer's parent company, American Media Inc. Allegedly, it was said that AMI had taken on a sensitive assignment at Donald Trump's behest, and gone after a lead, not with a publication intention, but an intention to cause it to disappear.

As instructed, the employee opened the safe, picked out some documents and tried for a long time to get the safe shut. After a series of calls, the safe was properly closed. Another employee said that later that same day, a disposal crew came and carried a volume of refuse that was way larger than the usual. As it stood, a document which concerned Trump, in addition to other documents which the Enquirer had hitherto possessed, had been shredded.

Now this is the real deal. Sometime in June 2016, Howard had gathered a bunch of dirt about Trump, which had carefully been stored and piled up in AMI's archives. When the elections were over, Trump's lawyer, Michael Cohen had made a request for all the tabloid's empire materials about the new president. While some resisted, knowing that surrendering it would result in a legally problematic paper trail, Howard and other senior members of staff instructed that the reporting materials which were not in the small safe be sent to AMI headquarters. When it arrived, it was initially placed in the small safe. However, as politics began to have its way, with the relationship between the magazine and the President getting frosty, the reporting material was moved to a bigger safe in the office of the head of human resources, Daniel Rotstein. At some point however, an employee began to get jumpy and decided to undertake a check. It was then that he found out that the list of Trump dirt did not tally with the physical files, as some of the materials had disappeared. Till today, however, Howard maintains that nothing was ever destroyed.

There are two sides to this. On one hand, the destruction of the documents would lend credence to a widely spread notion that had characterized the Enquirer, and the AMI for years. On a routine basis, the AMI blackmailed its employees, by withholding the publication of damaging information in exchange for tips. On the other hand, a new wave seemed to be taking over AMI's offices in Manhattan's Financial District. David Pecker, a graying former accountant from the Bronx had been friends with Trump for decades. As the years rolled by, they both enjoyed each other's friendship, to their mutual benefit. For Trump thought, the benefits were more consequential. It was alleged that Pecker must have put nothing less than ten stories to death for Trump. And as soon as Trump decided to run for office, loyalty deepened, and soon enough, the Enquirer and other AMI outlets endorsed Trump formally whilst screaming about Hilary Clinton's treachery and flagging health.

CHAPTER 4: BUTTON

KEY TAKEAWAYS

- Matt Lauer was paid more than twenty million dollars annually
- Matt Lauer was a firm advocate of investigative reporting.

I was meeting with Matt Lauer in his office on the third floor of 30, Rockefeller Plaza. He had gradually built his career, rising through the ladder from a local television in West Virginia to being one of the key figures in network television. He was paid more than twenty million dollars annually, in addition to being ferried to and from his house by helicopter. Lauer was making comments about my recent investigative series, referring to it as good stuff. He went on to ask questions that pertained to the stories. When I mentioned the Hanford nuclear facility, he responded by saying the show needed more of this kind of stuff. He was a firm advocate of investigative reporting.

He went on to ask what I had coming up next. I was still reeling out the different stories when his eyes snapped back to me with keen interest. I'm not sure which of the stories caught his attention, but he looked at me and said they sound terrific. Next up, he asked where I saw myself in the next few years. Truth is, I was proud of the work I was doing, but I continually struggled with carving a niche for myself. I had considered various options, but I remained unsatisfied. Responding to his question, I said I'd love to return to anchoring at some point in time. He looked me in the eye, telling me that's what I thought I wanted, but that deep down within him, he knew I was searching for something; something I'd have to figure out myself- something I deeply cared about. Smiling at me, he asked if I was excited about the next week. I was, honestly.

I had been scheduled to fill in when every other anchor, including Lauer himself, took a break for the Christmas holiday. He reminded me of all I needed to arm myself with- interaction, orange room tags, personalizing my scripts, and a host of others. I thanked him, while I took a few notes down. Soon after, he made for the door, but not without telling me not to let him down, as he would be watching the show.

Few weeks after I had a conversation with Lauer, I sat opposite the executive in charge of the Today show, Noah Oppenheim. Flanking me were McHugh and

Jackie Levin. Oppenheim proceeded to find out what I had, while I leaned back to give him an update. Like Lauer, he was a fan of hard news. Having being tapped to run Today, he came to meet with me, telling me to deal just with him, and none of the other executives at the show. More frequently, he'd put me on the Today show, thereby fueling my increasingly ambitious investigations. He was a great, smart guy who certainly knew his onions. After working with TV for a while, he ventured into the movie business, particularly screenwriting. Having left for quite a while, rates were dropping drastically, and the NBC had to bring him back to Today to resuscitate the show.

CHAPTER 5: KANDAHAR

KEY TAKEAWAYS

- I had always avoided my sister's allegation
- Rose McGowan predicted that there would be a battle over the male-controlled structures within Hollywood, and even beyond it.

Weinstein was in LA, meeting with Black Cube operatives. According to the operatives, they had been making good progress. Quickly, Weinstein's lawyers covered the last payment for the first part of the second phase, but for some reason, sat on an invoice for the concluding part for over a month. A lot of tense exchanges had to go on before they finally made payment, commencing the next, deeper, more intense stage of the operation.

For us at NBC, reporting had taken a more intense turn. In January, the Hollywood series took shape, as I began reporting a story on rigged awards campaigns, along with one about sexist hiring practices behind the camera and another about Chinese influence on American blockbusters. However, my story on sexual harassment proved an uphill task, as actress after actress continued to back out. Regardless, the calls kept picking a lot of information, and over and over, Harvey Weinstein's name kept coming up.

Dee Nickerson, a producer, arrived for an interview about the China story. As soon as she was done, I hurriedly went after her as she approached the nearest elevator. Immediately, I mentioned to her that we were working on a story about sexual harassment in the industry, and rhetorically asked if she used to work for Harvey Weinstein. Her smile went flat, as she responded that she couldn't be of help to me. Determined not to give up so easily, I asked if she had anyone in mind who I could speak with. She responded by saying she had a flight to catch. However, just as she got into the elevator, she paused and told me to be careful.

Few days afterwards, I placed a call across to Rose McGowan. We had met over lunch in 2010, and kicked off almost immediately. On this occasion in 2017, she picked my call from the newsroom. According to her, Roy Prince, Amazon's movie and TV studio head had greenlit a show she was creating regarding a cult. She predicted that there would be a battle over the male-controlled structures within Hollywood, and even beyond it. Talking from a political perspective, she zeroed in on what Hilary losing the election means to women all over the world. Going on and on, she spoke without reservation about everything, including the allegation she had lodged against Weinstein- one that said that Weinstein had raped her.

I proceeded to ask if she would be comfortable calling him out, on camera, to which she responded that she would think about it. At this point in time, she was working on a book and was considering what and what not to reveal. McGowan particularly mentioned that the media had rejected her, and she had done the same in return. Wondering why she then agreed to talk to me, she responded by saying that I had lived it, and that she saw what I wrote. This is where it gets interesting. A year before this meeting of ours, the Hollywood Reporter had published an amazing, incredible profile of my dad, sparingly mentioning the sexual allegations levelled against him by my younger sister, Dylan. The magazine suffered a lot of criticism for that piece, and the reporter's editor turned to me to write about whether the backlash was deserving, or not.

Now, for a long time, I had always avoided my sister's allegation, publicly and otherwise. I struggled to be me-undefined by my childhood, sister or even my parents. My mom suffered a great deal in the hand of men, and I made up my mind to be on my own, and become the best in my field, regardless of whatever it might cost me. And so, for the very first time in my life, I decided to interview my sister, who repeated the exact same thing she said when she was just seven years old. According to her, my dad had taken her to a space in our home, and penetrated her with his finger. Several other people including a therapist whom he hired and a baby sister came forward to corroborate Dylan's claims. Hence, when I wrote my piece, I made it clear that her claim had become one of the many sexual abuse allegations that remained often ignored by the news media, which in my opinion was not just wrong, but dangerous as well.

Hoping that this would be my one and only statement on the issue, I let it rest. However, McGowan made it clear to me that there really was no end to it.

CHAPTER 6: CONTINENTAL

KEY TAKEAWAYS

- Richard Greenberg, an NBC expert had been given the editorial position

On the show today, I had just tidied things up on a segment that concerned a battle between safety advocates and the trucking industry over whether to require side guards on tractor-trailers, to stop cars from slipping under them. While the safety advocates insisted that the move would save lives, the trucking industry complained about the expense involved. Just about that time, Matt Lauer commended me, saying that it was a good one with a good engagement. Upon thanking him, he asked about the other stories I was working on. I was unsure as to which one he as referring to, but is simply told him about the contaminated California farmlands, which I thought he would find interesting. As he walked out, he mentioned that if I did need anything, I could come to him, after which he left.

February 2017 was here. McHugh and I lay laden with meetings with the networks legal and standard departments, who were bent on scrutinizing every bit of the upcoming Hollywood stories. Richard

Greenberg, an NBC expert had been given the editorial position. Greenberg had become a veteran, having spent almost seventeen years at the NBC. He was a quiet, yet morally convicted individual.

When McHugh and I sat with Greenberg in his office that week, we outlined what our shooting schedule for the following week would involve. I mentioned a number of practices that were conversant with my investigative work. Next up, he asked if I had run through all of that with Chung, to which I responded in the affirmative. Right after, he turned to his computer system, pulled up a browser, and ran a search with my parent's names and Weinstein's. I thought to myself that this was a pretty good idea, as I had not thought of that myself. As expected, Weinstein had touched movies worked on by both my parents. Somehow though, I never heard his name from either of them.

After scrolling through, Greenberg said everything looked good and that he was just double-checking to be sure there was nothing in secret, which clearly, there wasn't.

Some days later, I sat in a hotel room with Dennis Rice, an expert marketing executive. At the beginning, we planned on discussing only the story on rigged award campaigns. Following this, I asked him about his time as Harvey Weinstein's president of marketing at Miramax in the late '90s and early 2000s, and he suddenly grew nervous, saying things would get tough on him if he dared say anything. However, he kinda realized that he might be helping with some extremely important piece of work, and therefore agreed to return for the follow- on interview.

Speaking about his time at Miramax, he explained that money was made available in the event that there was some carelessness that needed to be treated. Carelessness here includes bullying, sexual harassment and physical abuse. He confessed to having witnessed his boss touching young women inappropriately, an being paid off in the end. More grievous was their encouragement to keep their mouths sealed, or their careers would be brought to a halt. In addition, he admitted to knowing some specific cases of revenge. When the recording was over, he told me to go find Rosanna Arquette. Rosanna was an actress who came into the limelight with a major role in the movie titled Desperately Seeking Susan. While wiping sweat from his forehead, he concluded by hoping that she would be willing to talk.

CHAPTER 7: PHANTOMS

KEY TAKEAWAYS

- Noah Oppenheim had been promoted to president of NBC News.
- Rose McGowan was tired.

Heading towards my shoot, an announcement hit the wires. Here it is: Noah Oppenheim had been promoted to president of NBC News. Together with his boss, Andy Lacks, he was embarking on a whole lot of mind-blowing projects. The first order they launched was to appoint Megyn Kelly a new role at NBC. Excited at the good news, I texted Oppenheim my heartfelt congratulations. He replied with a cool kind of thank you.

I browsed through my contacts and rang my sister Dylan up. This was the first time I was calling her in months. I told her where I was headed, and that I was going to meet with a renowned actress who was accusing a powerful person of a serious crime. In all of our family photos, Dylan had always crouched behind me. I was quite surprised that she picked the call, 'cos she hardly had her phone with her. Truthfully, she had confessed that hearing the phone ring caused her heart to race. Worse still was hearing the voice of a man at the other end of the line. For this reason, she never had a job that involved handling lots of phone calls. She was good at what she did- a writer and a visual artist. Her work was deep. It was different. Her escape from this world was fantasy- fantasies ruled her entire person. She would write about all sorts, flipping through hundreds of pages of fictions. Yet, they never got published, but instead, he stored them all away in her drawer. I always pushed that she submits a manuscript, but she never agreed to it. Rather than do that, she'd come up defensive, telling me I didn't never understand.

While still on the phone with her, she asked if I wanted her advice. I responded in the affirmative. She told me that this was the worst part of the entire thing- the consideration and the wait for the story. She then added that once you voice out, it becomes much easier. She said to tell the actress in question to hang tough. Lastly, she told me that if I got this, I shouldn't let it go.

Rose McGowan lived in one of those typical-movie-star houses, with a lot of beautiful descriptions to adorn it. Sitting across her, she looked very different. Pretty different from the woman I met seven years back. This Rose McGowan looked tired. She had a hard tension across her face. She was dressed in a loose beige sweater, and wore little makeup. Her hair was shaved.

McGowan had it rough in her childhood. Where she grew up, women were strict and men were ruthless. She once told me that when she was about four years of age, one man had sliced a wart off her finger without warning, leaving her to bleed. At some point, she was a homeless teenager. Thus, having made it in Hollywood, she assumed she was beyond being exploited. But she was wrong.

Her business manager has set up the meeting where she was allegedly assaulted by Weinstein. According to her, things had abruptly been moved from a hotel restaurant to a hotel suite. In the first hour, he was praising her and commending her performance in scream, and Phantoms. Still in that state, she was shocked when everything moved from being a meeting. And before she knew it, her clothes were taken off her. I began to cry. She admitted to this being both a sexual assault and rape, and said that she considered pressing criminal charges. To her utmost surprise, the attorney had rebuffed her saying she had done a sex scene and that no one was ever going to believe her. Deciding not to press charges anymore, she signed away her right to sue Weinstein for a hundred thousand dollars, which she considered a lot of money at the time.

CHAPTER 8: GUN

KEY TAKEAWAYS

- The reporting grew bigger and bigger each passing day.
- Before now, no one seemed to have taken Weinstein up.

I sent a text to Oppenheim, telling him how shocking the interview with Rose was. He went 'wow'. I continued describing the event in detail, adding that the interview would be fun for legal. Again, he responded saying it definitely would.

After we finished our shoot for the day, McHugh and I placed calls across to Greenberg, the head of the investigative unit, and Chung, the attorney. Before then, I had spoken with two persons on McGowan's management team whom she had complained to immediately after meeting with Weinstein.

McHugh and I returned to our hotel in Santa Monica with the aim of interviewing a Chinese filmmaker. Speaking with Greenberg, I mentioned that McGowan said she'll give us the contract she had with Weinstein. He cut me short right there, ordering me to be careful about that. McHugh proceeded to find out what he meant by that statement. He simply responded by saying he didn't know that we could be interfering with contracts.

Frustrated, McHugh spoke. He was passionate about us running this story. He considered it big news, an outright explosive. Greenberg however saw things differently. While he did not try to water down the huge nature of the story at hand, he mentioned that he did not see it being ready in time for the series. Actually, they were due to run in one week. I chipped in saying that I could get other women to talk in time, just before it airs, but Greenberg asked that I give the story the time and attention it deserved, explaining that other stories could air for now. I didn't mind though, as long as the delay was being used to create a better, stronger reporting.

The reporting grew bigger and bigger. The following day after shooting with McGowan, we arrived at the offices of the Hollywood Reporter to interview one of their journalists on the awards beat- Scot Feinberg. It was impossible to avoid mentioning Weinstein's name here too, since he was more or less the brain behind the Oscar campaign of today. And before I left the

Hollywood Reporter, I met with its editor who was new at the time. His name was Matt Belloni. I had heard a lot about his predecessor who convinced me to write about the need for tougher coverage of sexual assault allegations. Particularly, I heard that he had gone after the Weinstein allegation for years, but arrived at nothing, since no one was willing talk. However, Belloni had some ideas about key figures in the industry that might be aware of other women with such allegations. He made a suggestion to call Gavin Polone- a former agent, and manager, who had become a producer and was well known with his reputation as firebrand. Polone had in 2014 written a piece for the Hollywood Reporter titled "Bill Cosby and Hollywood's Culture of Payoffs, Rape and Secrecy." In this piece, he made reference to a particular studio head that over time used his money and power to silence allegations against him. He equally accused journalists of avoiding the story for fear of being sued and loss of adverts. It appeared therefore that before now, no one seemed to have taken Weinstein up.

CHAPTER 9: MINIONS

KEY TAKEAWAYS

- Gutierrez was a highly organized person.

- Weinstein was never charged as the attorney turned the case on Gutierrez

I arrived at Gramercy Traven to meet Gutierrez sitting and waiting for me. She was a highly organized individual who grew up seeing her father beat her mom. If she ever tried to intervene, she got beat up as well. Very early on in life, she became the caretaker in her house, providing support for her mother whilst distracting her brother from the violence in their home. She was beautiful, very beautiful. Meeting with me, she said she wanted to be of help, but that she was in a difficult situation. It was only when I told her that some other woman had opened up on camera, and that many others were willing to tow the same line that she began to talk.

In 2015, her modelling agent invited her over to a reception at Radio City Music Hall for a show that Weinstein produced. As was characteristic of him, Weinstein had pulled all his strings in the industry to garner support for and towards the show. Steve Burke, the CEO of NBC Universal had agreed to provide costumes of characters from the ubiquitous Minions franchise.

While at the reception, Weinstein could not take his eyes off Gutierrez. Approaching her, he told her that she looked like the actress, Mila Kunis. Later that day, she received a mail from her agency stating that Weinstein wanted to set up a business meeting with her as soon as possible. In high spirits, she arrived at his office the next evening with her modelling portfolio. As they both sat on the couch whilst reviewing her portfolio, he began to stare at her breasts, and then, plunged at her, grabbing her breasts while attempting to dip his hands into her skirt. She resisted him, he backed off and the told her that his assistant would give her tickets to Finding Neverland later that night.

She never attended the show, but instead went to the nearest police station to lodge a complaint. Weinstein was upset that she did not attend the show. While on a call with him, investigators devised a plan to have her wear a wire, attend the show the next day and tactically get him to confess. She did get him to confess to groping her the day before- a full, dramatic confession. However, Weinstein was never charged as the attorney turned the case on her, digging into her past and labeling her a prostitute. Eventually, she signed off her right to talk publicly about Weinstein for a million dollars.

Still obviously shaken by the incident, she said she realized her decision was wrong the minute she did it. But she took the money to help her mother and brother. Following this, she came down with depression and an eating disorder, and her brother had to come see her in the States. He then took her to Italy so she could start her life all over again.

CHAPTER 10: MAMA

KEY TAKEAWAYS

- Gutierrez had signed a million-dollar nondisclosure agreement.
- I was in in touch with five different women who all accused Weinstein of sexual misconduct.

Two years after our meeting, Gutierrez still wrestled with the memory of the incident. I asked if she had the document, and promised to use it only in a way that was comfortable for her. Picking up a white iPhone, she began to click and scroll. After a while, she pushed the phone my way, allowing me go through the million-dollar nondisclosure agreement she signed.

It was a long one, eighteen pages long. On the last page, both Gutierrez and Weinstein had their signatures. I like to think that the lawyers who put it together must have been so certain that it would never leak. The terms of the contract included the destruction of all copies of audio recordings of Weinstein admitting to the groping. Gutierrez also consented to hand over her phone, as well as other devices which might have contained evidence to Kroll, a private-security firm retained by Weinstein. In addition, she surrendered the passwords to her email accounts and other forms of digital communication that could have been used to spirit out copies. An attorney once remarked that the Weinstein agreement was one of the deadliest, he had ever seen in all his years of practice. A sworn statement which Gutierrez had signed previously stated in detail that the behavior Weinstein agreed to in the recording was false. This statement was also attached to the document.

Looking up from the agreement and my transcription notepad, I asked her if all copies of the tapes were destroyed. They weren't all destroyed. I left the restaurant, and headed towards McHugh, and told him all that had just happened. I mentioned the existence of the audio as well. Texting Oppenheim, I relayed all that happened, including the fact that I was now in touch with five different women who all accused Weinstein of sexual misconduct. When Oppenheim replied much later, the only thing he asked was who my producer was.

McHugh and I returned to the Plaza and went to Greenberg's office. He did admit that this was a hell of a story, after which he moved towards his monitor, and typed Gutierrez's name into the system. Scrolling through a few of her pictures where she lay seductively in lingerie, he did say she did not look bad. At all.

I turned to Greenberg and told him that we were about to hit a major piece of evidence, as Gutierrez had said she would play the audio for me. He just responded that we'd see about that. Immediately, McHugh chipped in about the contract, to which Greenberg responded that it was complicated. I said to him that we were not making her do anything.

Later that same afternoon, I placed a call across to Chung, the NBC lawyer. Chung explained that on a theoretical scale, someone could have induced her to violate the contract. However, a tort like that would be considered weird, as there exist lots of interpretations that conflict with another, as to what is required to prove it.

CHAPTER 11: BLOOM

KEY TAKEAWAYS

- I met with Gutierrez, again.
- Harvey Weinstein had been calling Boies, his attorney, about Rose McGowan.

Meeting with Gutierrez a second time caused me to be late for drinks with an assistant to my former boss at MSNBC, Phil Griffin. I warned her ahead in a text though that because of the nature of the story I was working on, I might be late. I was still apologizing when I got to the restaurant where we agreed to meet. Asking her how Griffin was doing made her laugh, for he had asked the same about me.

Griffin was the one person who believed in me, and gave me a shot by bringing me into the NBC. Very diligent and talented human, he had gradually worked his way up to the top by taking up role at CNN, the Today show and the Nightly News. He had focused on sports at CNN, and was greatly interested and passionate about baseball. He was magnanimous enough not to rob my incomprehension about the sport in my face. At the MSNBC, he was in charge of the cable channel's greatest periods, and somehow managed to survive its bad times. Ever since my show got cancelled, the only thing that ever brought us together was cordial office run-ins.

Harvey Weinstein had been calling Boies, his attorney, about Rose McGowan since shortly after she tweeted the previous fall. However, he had never mentioned NBC until that spring. According to him, he knew that the NBC was doing a story, wanting to know if Boies had any information on the matter. Boies replied in the negative. And it was only a couple of days again before he called asking the same question.

Weinstein repeatedly called his lawyers about news outlets pursuing troublesome stories for years. This was however different as he began to tell all those around him that information was reaching him directly from the NBC. Soon enough, he began to talk about the worth of the network, and the reporter who was working on the story. Gutierrez and I continued to meet up, as she grappled with whether or not to release the evidence.

At a point, I had to call my sister Dylan for advice again. I explained the whole situation on ground to her. After thinking for a moment, she said that I should call Lisa Bloom- a lawyer who also acted as one on TV, but mainly uses her platform for the purpose of defending her clients and protecting survivors of sexual violence who confronted the rich and powerful.

CHAPTER 12: FUNNY

KEY TAKEAWAYS

- Gutierrez had agreed to meet with our legal department, and present the evidence.
- Harvey Weinstein had called earlier in the day.

McHugh and I sat in Greenberg's office, feeding him up-to-date on the events with Gutierrez. I mentioned to him that she had agreed to meet with our legal department, and present the evidence before them. In my opinion, I said that it would be best to schedule this before she began to develop cold feet. However, he didn't oblige to the meeting, insisting that we needed to be armed with the audio, instead of merely having it played for us. I agreed with him, but insisted that more than anything, Gutierrez was willing to share it with us, and that meeting with the NBC might be some form of persuasion. Again, he raised a concern that examining contracts might invite some form of liability, still insisting that we had to run each and every one of these by legal. I was still reminding him that I had not done any of these without legal being in the know when his phone rang.

Dropping the call, he turned to McHugh and I, and said that was Harvey Weinstein, and that he had called earlier in the day. Shocked to our marrows, McHugh and I exchanged glances. This was entirely new to us. According to Greenberg, Weinstein had pressed for details about the story, and that he had begun with flattery, saying how much he was a fan of mine and a fan of the network. Later on, he resorted to saber-rattling, where he mentioned having retained some lawyers. Curiously, I asked if Weinstein was referring to David Boies, but Greenberg responded by saying that Boies was mentioned, but beyond Boies, there was Charles Harder. Now, Harder was the attorney who billionaire Peter Thiel, in an invasion of privacy case he bankrolled, had prevailed in successfully to shut down the gossip news site, Gawker.

Greenberg said that he responded to him telling him he could not discuss specific details, and would rather do this by the books.

As I sat at my desk early in April, I received a text from Matthew Hiltzik who was a prominent publicist. Soon after, he was ringing my cell asking all sorts of 'how are you doing?' questions. If there was one thing I knew, it was that Hiltzik never called without a purpose, and I was determined to find out why he was calling me. It did not take too long to find out as he began to make sarcastic comments about what stories I was working on. Shortly after, he asked if what I was working on was for the NBC, and I simply responded that I was an investigative correspondent for the NBC. He pressed further to find out if this was about Rose McGowan, stating categorically that Weinstein had said he could clear that up. I carefully chose my words, and told him that I welcomed any relevant information. Two hours after, he texted saying Weinstein was upset and agitated, but that he doubted he was going to be taking any action.

CHAPTER 13: DICK

KEY TAKEAWAYS

- Someone else had tried to nail Weinstein more recently
- Weinstein did not deny the allegations.

If there was anything I deduced from my call with Hiltzik, it was that someone else had tried to nail Weinstein more recently. Quickly, I sent a message to Jennifer Senior, the writer who worked with Carr. I asked her to find out if anyone else was working on the story, more recently than David Carr had. She wrote back to me saying that someone had, but for some reason, she decided against disclosing the writer. Apparently, things had ended poorly. Sadly, I told her to pass on a message to the mystery writer.

Ken Auletta, a write with The New Yorker was well known for his thorough appraisals of business and media executives. Auletta, in 2002, profiled Weinstein. In his piece, he dwelt on Weinstein's brutality, although he made no reference, or at most, no explicit pointer to sexual predation. He described Weinstein as coarse and threatening, and there was a hint in the piece that suggested there was more to what was being told. I sent a mail requesting for Auletta's email address.

At the time, Auletta was seventy-five years old. His carriage and speech were different, and he made a very fine reporter. When I called him, he did say that there was more to the story than he was able to print. As far back as 2002, Auletta had also laid claims that said that Weinstein was preying on women, and had once asked about the allegations in an interview. Both Weinstein and Auletta had been sitting in the former's office. Livid, Weinstein stood to his feet, and asked Auletta if he was trying to get his wife to divorce him. Fully prepared to beat the crap out of Weinstein, Auletta also stood to his feet. However, Weinstein gently sat down, and began to sob. He did not deny the allegations, but instead he said that he might not always be on his best behavior, but that he did love his wife.

CHAPTER 14: ROOKIE

KEY TAKEAWAYS

- Weinstein tried to discredit each and every woman who he had come at.

It was the 24th of April, and three men were seated at Weinstein's usual table near the kitchen in the back of the Tribeca Grill. These three men were Weinstein, Dylan Howard and an operative from the Black Cube.

Shortly afterwards, Lanny Davis walked into the room, surveying the entire room. Davis was already in his early seventies. Weinstein met Davis at an event honoring Hillary Clinton and knew of the crisis manager's familiarity with the sexual misconduct allegations against Bill Clinton. He enlisted Davis that spring.

That morning, Davis made mention that they could not speak in the presence of the Black Cube operative if Weinstein wanted to maintain attorney-client privilege, remarking that he could not speak in front of people who were not attorneys. This upset Weinstein who insisted, causing Davis to relent.

Weinstein went on and on, calling McGowan a crazy liar. What he tried to do was discredit each and every woman who he had come at, describing all of their accusations as false. Davis told Weinstein not to tow that line, even if he did think he was in the right, but Weinstein began to ask why. Davis responded that it looked awful. Dylan Howard grinned, but the Black cube operative didn't. Few hours after the meeting, Dr. Avi Yanus, Black Cube's director and CFO, sent an email to Weinstein's attorneys at Boies Schiller Flexner, describing the meeting as productive. According to the mail that was sent, the Black cube was committed to ensuring that their intelligence was brought to bear in the case, and most importantly, achieve all of their main objectives.

CHAPTER 15: STATIC

KEY TAKEAWAYS

- Jennifer Senior introduced me to Ben Wallace
- Wallace took the high road and shredded all of his notes

Like she had promised, Jennifer Senior introduced me to Ben Wallace, the mystery New York magazine writer who made a recent attempt at the Weinstein story. That afternoon, I placed a call across to him as I left the Plaza. He did not hesitate to tell me just how frustrating the assignment had been for him. Anything he got wind of somehow had a way of getting back to Weinstein. He referred to everyone as being a double agent. This was particularly true about the sources that had offered to help out. He suspected that Anna was hiding something, even though she was the one who told him she had a story about Weinstein. He said not only did he find some of her questions strange, he found it suspicious that she wanted to know the other sources and people he was working with.

As a matter of fact, the amount of information she wanted to squeeze out of him was in no way proportionate to what she was offering him. Her story with Weinstein was nothing concrete. According to her, they both had an affair that ended poorly and she wanted to take revenge. That was it. But while she recounted her story about Weinstein, she dangled her wrist in front of him, giving Wallace had a prickly suspicion that she might be secretly recording. Being professional about the whole event, Wallace sympathized with her but said he did consider consensual affairs to be Weinstein's private business; after which he left the hotel and stopped picking her calls.

He felt the same way about Seth Freedman, from whom he never got any meaningful information. Because he was suspicious too, Wallace cut ties there as well. Soon after, Weinstein's associates began to call the New York magazine, threatening to divulge personal information about Wallace. Weinstein requested, or better still, demanded for a meeting between his legal team, investigators from Kroll, and the magazine. But the magazine declined the meeting.

This experience did put Wallace on the edge. And with the incessant amount of calls from Weinstein and his team, Wallace took the high road and shredded all of his notes.

CHAPTER 16: F.O.H

KEY TAKEAWAYS

- Ben Wallace was following up with the former assistant who had now decide he would talk to me.
- Emily worried that the casual, practiced nature of the harassment was a pattern.

The next ring on my phone had good news as Ben Wallace was following up with the former assistant who had now decide he would talk to me. The week after, I walked into a Beverly Hills Hotel. Recognizing my source, she grinned at me and introduced herself as Emily.

Her name was Emily Nestor, and she held law and business degrees from Pepperdine. At the moment she worked for a tech startup, but she still seemed to be on the lookout for something more fulfilling. She had once wanted to be in film business, but while she worked as a temporary assistant, her belief in the business was shaken. She worried that the casual, practiced nature of the harassment was a pattern. Worse still, the response she got when she reported it left her in total disarray.

Without further ado, I went straight to what we had on ground: McGowan and Gutierrez named in the story, and the audio, and the increasing amount of executives on camera. I was honest about everything to her. She appeared scared as she told me she'd think about it. She was scared of retaliating. But I also noticed that her convictions were so strong, and that they would not go away that easily.

Few days after we met, she was in, and agreed to go on camera, although she preferred to remain anonymous, and hidden within the shadow to start out, and much later, she'd see about how she felt going further. She had huge evidence- solid evidence.

I spoke to McHugh about Noah making sure that the story was aired if we could get this to him. Soon after, Nestor, McHugh and myself started out our shoot. With her face deepened into shadow, Nestor said she anticipated a personal and vengeful response from Weinstein when he saw the story. He had worked at the Weinstein company in LA at the age of twenty five as a temporary front desk assistant. She knew she was overqualified for the job, but she took it so as to get a firsthand view of the entertainment industry. Her first day at work had two employees telling her how much of Weinstein's type she was, physically. Weinstein did not fall short of what they had said, as he continually referred to her as the pretty girl. He asked her how old she was, sent his assistants out of the room and had her write her telephone number down. He invited her to drinks that night, but she came up with an excuse as to why she couldn't. Because he insisted, she suggested coffee the next morning. He accepted, and they did meet. He began to offer her career help, telling her about his escapades with several women. Nestor continually witnessed him yelling into his cellphone and spin things around in his favor. Upon completing her temporary placement, Nestor left the firm traumatized, and decided against going into entertainment because of this incident.

CHAPTER 17: 666

KEY TAKEAWAYS

- On June 6, operatives of the Black cube met with Weinstein and his lawyers at Boies Schiller.
- Sometime in July, Black Cube and Boies revised their agreement.

While Weinstein's former employees talked to me, he talked to Black Cube. On June 6, operatives of the Black cube met with Weinstein and his lawyers at Boies Schiller in New York. There, they delivered a high-spirited update. At the end of the meeting, Black Cube Director, Yanus, checked in with Boies. Yanus stated how much a pleasure it had been meeting with Boies and Weinstein, whilst presenting the final report. Attaching a six hundred dollars invoice, Yanus commended the Black cube team for having successfully achieved the project's objectives and met all three success fee divisions. According to him, the most important clause was identifying who stood behind the negative campaign against the client.

One week passed and Yanus checked in once again to find out the state of things with the payment. Once again, he got no response. Weinstein sat on the invoice, straining his rapport with the Black cube.

Occasionally, Yanus would call in and simply state that they were yet to be paid. And while sometimes Weinstein would feign ignorance, at other times he would yell at Yanus as to why he should pay them. Things got to a head in June when Weinstein raised a question about Black Cube's work breaking the law, thereby leaving him exposed to problems down the road. He was livid as he explained that the operation did not completely solve his problems.

Finally, sometime in July, Black Cube and Boies revised their agreement. Weinstein agreed to pay a one hundred and ninety-thousand-dollar settlement to square away the unpleasantness about the success fees. And Black Cube signed on to a new schedule of work, through November of that year, with a new, more targeted set of goals.

CHAPTER 18: QUIDDITCH

KEY TAKEAWAYS

- There were varying layers of concrete evidence and credible sources
- We were going to have to make the case to the lawyers that this is worth it.

Noah Oppenheim appeared speechless. I gave him a printed list of the reporting elements. He exclaimed wow, adding that it was a lot to digest. Outside his office window, sunlight fell across Rockefeller Plaza.

I explained to Noah that we had varying layers of concrete evidence and credible sources. As a matter of fact, some of them even knew Oppenheim. Oppenheim lifted the uppermost page once more and turned to look at the one underneath. Putting the paper down on his lap, he sighed and said we were going to have to make certain decisions. Decisions? I was confused. I wondered if this was really worth it.

I turned to look at Oppenheim, and told him this was a big story. I continued, adding that this was about a prominent figure who admitted to committing sexual misconduct, on tape! He responded by saying he wasn't sure if that was a crime, to which I said it's a misdemeanor and that potentially, it meant some jail time. Next up, he said we'd have to decide if it's newsworthy. I was blank! I stared at him. He spoke again, saying we both knew who "Harvey Weinstein is. I know who Harvey Weinstein was particularly because we were both in the industry, and that there was no guarantee that the average American knew who he was. I tried so hard to explain why this had every reason to be out there, by the simply said that we were going to have to make the case to the lawyers that this is worth it.

Recalling Wallace's reactions, I knew Oppenheim was right about this. Leaving him, I walked out cracking a silly joke about an accident befalling me. He laughed, and tapped the paper I'd handed him saying he'd make sure it got out.

CHAPTER 19: SPIRAL

KEY TAKEAWAYS

- I put a call across to Auletta telling him I had more information regarding settlements in London.
- Far back as fifteen years ago, there were actually notes that covered great ground about the issue.

Later that July, I put a call across to Auletta telling him I had more information regarding settlements in London. In addition, I asked if there was anything else he could show me to help beef up my reporting. Surprisingly, he responded in the affirmative. Apparently, he had provided all his reporters with notebooks, printed documents, and tapes to the New York Public Library. The collection here remained closed to members of the public. However, he said I could take a look.

McHugh and I signed into the library, while a librarian brought out all of Auletta's boxes. We each took a box and began devouring their contents. Auletta didn't have nearly as much as we did. But he had grasped at essential pieces of the puzzle. It was very strange that far back as fifteen years ago, there were actually notes that covered such ground. Yet, even then, Auletta encountered a lot of abandoned reporting jobs. He scribbled on a page of notes- David Carr: believes sexual harassment.

In his collection of reporter's notebooks, I found clues that led to other clues, fusing my evolving picture of what had happened between Weinstein and the two assistants in London. This is it. In the late nineties, Perkins was working as an assistant to Gigliotti, which in the real state of things translated to working mostly for Weinstein. Later on, she told me that from the first time she was left alone with Weinstein, she had to contend with him being either in his underpants or totally naked, trying to pull her into bed. Perkins was small and flaxen. She did look a lot younger than her age. But she was also vert sharp and assertive. And never for once did Weinstein succeed in his physical advances towards her. She was however exhausted from his unending attempts. And soon enough, he began to wear her down in other ways. And like many of Weinstein's former employees, she found herself becoming as a facilitator of sexual associations with aspiring actresses and models, basically bringing girls to him. Initially, she said she wasn't aware of it. Weinstein would use her, asking her to buy condoms for him and clean up the hotel-room after his meetings with the young women.

It was not until 1998 that Perkins got the go-ahead to hire her own assistant, as she earnestly hoped that this would put some distance between herself and Weinstein. As candidates applied for the role, she warned them that Weinstein would make sexual advances. She went as far as rejecting very overtly attractive applicants because she knew he'd go after them. Finally, she chose Chiu, a bright, Oxford graduate, who would overcome crippling fears of revenge and make her name public years later.

CHAPTER 20: CULT

KEY TAKEAWAYS

- McHugh had first-hand information about Weinstein having misappropriated funds meant for charity.
- Susan said she did not see any outstanding legal issues based on her review of the material.

We had put a script together over the course of late July, which I would describe as economical. The script consisted of the tape, McGowan's on-camera interview and Nestor's face hidden in shadow interview, alongside images of her messages from Irwin Reiter which revealed just how much of a problem Weinstein's behavior was within the firm. We also included the evidence we had found from the two settlements in London as well as the check from Bon Weinstein's account. In addition to all these, the sound bites from the four former employees were also there. During this period, McHugh had also stumbled on some piece of information through a friend who had given him first-hand information about Weinstein having misappropriated funds meant for charity, and trying to get them to sign nondisclosure agreements.

The last week of July had Susan Weiner, the general counsel of NBC News, Greenberg, McHugh and myself sit in Greenberg's office, where she admitted that we had a lot, and that the next step would be to seek comment, expressing that she did not see any outstanding legal issues based on her review of the material.

Later that day, we all sat with Oppenheim in his office where we gave him the script to look through. Seeing his countenance, I mentioned that it was only a draft script and that I'd make it tighter. Greenberg suggested that Oppenheim listen to the audio, as Oppenheim's lack of enthusiasm seemed to be a bother to him. After listening to the tape, Oppenheim said he did not know what that proved. I responded, telling him he admits to groping her, but instead, he said that Weinstein was only trying to get rid of her. We tried for so long, but Oppenheim maintained his position- he did not think that this was newsworthy; neither did he believe that the American audience were in touch with who Weinstein was. He added that he didn't know if we could show contracts. We all left confused, wondering why a news organization which reported contractually protected information routinely in national security and business contexts, would take up sudden concern about settlements that had to do with sexual harassment. However, I made a point of note to tell him that the story would make big impact on whatever platform it got aired.

CHAPTER 21: SCANDAL

KEY TAKEAWAYS

- Greenberg told me that the story was currently under review by NBC Universal, and not NBC News.
- The story was now in the hands of the top executives at the NBC Universal and its parent company, Comcast.

Not too long after my meeting with Oppenheim, I made my way towards the East Village. McGowan and I had agreed to meet at the Airbnb where she was staying. Talking to her, I made mention of the fact that we currently had much stronger material, but that I was going to need her voice as it was highly important. What I really wanted to do was to take her suggestion that we have more shoots, and her offer to name Weinstein to the NBC lawyers. She responded, saying she did not trust the NBC. I carefully responded to this, saying that I know that they would do right by the story. Afterwards, she agreed to do it.

A few days after, she agreed to shoot a follow-up interview. But first of all, she had to go replace Val Kilmer at Tampa Bay Comic Con first. I thought it would be fun, and in fact, I said it out loudly, but she didn't think so, and she did not hide her opinion.

I returned to work, and was in the cafeteria when I got a call from Greenberg. I was about reeling out all about my experience with Rose later in the day when he asked if I could talk. I met with him in his office and aid all I had to say about my update with Rose McGowan. After I was done babbling, Greenberg told me that the story was currently under review by NBC Universal, and not NBC News. This simply meant that the story had gone upstairs, and was now in the hands of the top executives at the NBC Universal and its parent company, Comcast. He added however, that it was under legal review. Asking what they based this review on since no one had asked us for additional copies of material, or for the audio, he responded that he did not know too.

I thought to send the tape to Kim, but Greenberg refused saying we'd respect the process and remain at arm's length, and that he would ensure that Susan sends them whatever they need. I simply told him I'd keep him updated with the follow-up interview. Then I got a shocker- we were supposed to pause all reporting. I blurted out how difficult it had been having had Rose hang in there at all. And all of a sudden, he was asking me to cancel. Again, he responded simply by saying he never asked me to cancel, and that all he said was that I should pause.

CHAPTER 22: PATHFINDER

KEY TAKEAWAYS

- Oppenheim would not budge.
- McHugh and I agreed to reschedule with McGowan

McHugh had just texted me about our decision to keep our mouths shut, knowing that we had done out best to push Oppenheim, but he would not budge. However, there was still the tricky proposition of the shoot with McGowan and the order to cancel it.

McHugh asked if Noah had told me not to go ahead with the interview. I said he did. McHugh and I were beginning to accept that we might have to reschedule with McGowan, the risks involved notwithstanding. I put a call across to McGowan, and despite how much I tried to calm her down, I could feel the uncertainty building up within her. I went on to tell her that we could shoot at her place in LA, and that if all she could offer was Tuesday, then Tuesday it was.

The next morning, I repeatedly placed calls across to Kim Harris. Finally, she responded via email. stating that she'd been traveling for several days. She then suggested that we could meet the following week. However, this would not be in time for the McGowan interview. I pleaded with her, explaining that cancelling could cost us everything. On my part, I offered to brief Harris beforehand, letting her state what my posture in the interview would be. as I'd done with Chung. I then proceeded to call Weiner, after which I left her a voicemail where I made the same points again.

As I hung up, Greenberg invited me into his office. He said he called Weinstein back. Shocked at what I was hearing, I asked him to repeat himself. He said he told Weinstein that legal was vetting the script, and hence, nothing was running in the mean- time. According to him, Weinstein said he wanted to send a letter to the legal department of the NBC. Greenberg directed him to Susan Weiner. Giving me a heads up, he added that Weinstein may accuse me of maligning. I burst into laughter, while Greenberg remained serious. Responding to Greenberg, I said that I'd stand by anything I've said or put in writing. Greenberg advised that I be careful. I asked him if he had any information on the McGowan interview. All he said was that legal was still deciding if it could go ahead.

Soon after, I got a response from legal, as they had decided they would allow the interview proceed the following week. However, it was too late. McGowan just texted right about the same time about her inability to be in the segment, as the legal angle was coming for her.

CHAPTER 23: CANDY

KEY TAKEAWAYS

- Harris remarked that the story had elements of a tortious interference

In the first week of August, I arrived at Harris's office. I declined a call from my mother as I arrived, sending her a text to say a prayer. Truth is I'd broken rank to contact Harris and she hadn't added anyone to our emails. A few minutes later however, Greenberg arrived. He was soon followed by Weiner.

In the room, there was a vast difference between both women. Weiner was quiet and bureaucratic, while Harris exuded charisma. I wasn't surprised though, as she had graduated from the best institutions in the Ivy League, and more particularly, in the sequence required to achieve maximum status. She'd worked in the Obama White House and as a partner at a top-ranked firm. Much faster was she than both Greenberg and Weiner, and she had very little tolerance for ceremony.

Harris was the kind of lawyer one shouldn't joke with-highly sophisticated that you might miss her doing the work at all. Pulling out a copy of the script, she remarked that the story had elements of tortious interference.   I kept mute, even though I knew very well that this was complete nonsense.   Still, it felt reassuring to talk to Harris. From a legal standpoint, all she wanted me to do was to separate myself from the news division's editorial decision, and not to stand down. She requested that I produce another script, with the corrections having been effected.

As I left the building some hours later, I ran into Weiner. It was raining heavily outside, and to my utter surprise, she looked at me squarely and ordered me to keep moving. At some point, with pressure mounting on the story, McHugh and I began to drift apart. He was upset he wasn't a part of the meeting with Harris, wondering where my loyalties lay.

CHAPTER 24: PAUSE

KEY TAKEAWAYS

- Ally Canosa confirmed that she was fully aware she'd been aware of the honeypot meetings
- Ally Canosa was also sexually abused by Harvey Weinstein

Ally Canosa had worked for Weinstein since 2010. She confirmed almost immediately that she was fully aware she'd been aware of the honeypot meetings. In addition, she mentioned being sexually abused by Harvey Weinstein. I took a risk and showed her my cards, which caused her to break down in tears as she realized that the truth was finally going to come out. I asked if she'd be willing to go on camera. She sounded scared, but she welcomed the idea.

She agreed to meet me in Los Angeles in person. That weekend, she was available. I began to book a ticket almost immediately, but halted. Greenberg had just recently issued his latest order for me to stop reporting, and this time, he was invoking the legal department. Again, McHugh suggested that rather than asking for permission, I should ask for forgiveness.

I couldn't go rogue, so I called Weiner and told her the interview was important. I then sent an email pleading for permission to continue reporting. I didn't get a reply. I waited a day, after which I booked my ticket to LA.

Just as I was about to leave for the airport, I received a call from Greenberg. He said he had to get Susan on the phone. Immediately she joined, she carefully and slowly said that the company would like to put a pause on all reporting and contact with sources. I told them I didn't understand. I then questioned if this was an order from legal, to which Susan replied that it wasn't. Instead, she categorically stated that this was a direct order from Noah. At that instant, I attempted to make it clear that if legal hadn't determined that I stop reporting and Noah did, why didn't anyone express a rationale as to why it would place us in jeopardy to allow reporting to continue? I asked if he provided reasons for his order, and Susan stuttered saying that one might want to review what we, already have now before we continue with anything new. Stubbornly, I told her that the meeting definitely wasn't new, and that I had scheduled it.

CHAPTER 25: PUNDIT

KEY TAKEAWAYS

- Ally Canosa had signed a nondisclosure agreement.

Ally Canosa was a pretty lady who was unsure of what to do.as a condition of her employment with Weinstein; she had signed a nondisclosure agreement. She was still struggling to make a name as a producer, and was extremely terrified of revenge. Common, Weinstein could cost her being employable. In addition, there were the indecisions of any survivor of sexual violence. She'd permitted her wounds to harden and learned to move on. She told no one. Not her father, nor her boyfriend. She simply told me she didn't want to suffer more. Once, she garnered enough courage to approach a therapist who was a producer on one of Harvey's movies.

Canosa had met Weinstein when she was employed as an event planner at the West Hollywood branch of the members-only club Soho House. She'd planned an occasion for the Weinstein Company, and he'd spotted her, gazed, and then handed her his business card. Initially, Weinstein nearly trailed Canosa, demanding to meet over and over. When she was frightened, and didn't respond, he demanded a formal meeting through Soho House, supposedly to discuss another event. At the hotel, their meeting which was scheduled for midday was moved to a hotel suite. As usual, Weinstein laid into her with his usual promises of career advancement followed by sexual overtures. For a while, she tried to ignore him, but he kept coming after her. She lived in fear of the effect he might have on her profession if she snubbed him. Hence, she agreed to meet again.

The first year they worked together, Canosa tried so hard to ward off Weinstein's advances. During one meeting, he nonchalantly told her he had to go up to his hotel room to get something. When they arrived, he said he was going to take a shower, and asked if she would shower with him. He kept asking her to get in the shower with him, and that he had no intentions of having sex with her. She refused again, and left for the living room. From the bathroom, Weinstein said that that he was going to masturbate and began to do so through the open door. She left his hotel room, upset.

At another time, Weinstein left a jacket behind and asked her to hold onto it. In its pockets were packs of syringes that were a treatment for erectile dysfunction. She was disgusted at the mere thought of him building up himself for sex in advance of their meetings.

Soon after this incident, he raped her. The second time, Weinstein didn't use protection. She was terrified he might have infected her with an STD. She said she did think of telling her boyfriend, but was too ashamed to do so.

CHAPTER 26: BOY

KEY TAKEAWAYS

- George Pataki informed Weinstein that Ronan Farrow was still working on the story

A call came in from George Pataki, the former New York governor for Weinstein. He had called to inform Weinstein that Ronan Farrow was still working on the story. Weinstein responded saying that wasn't what he heard. According to Pataki, numerous females were speaking to me.

Weinstein was definitely not more interested in politics anywhere else than he was in New York. Between 1999 and 2017, his company had given to nothing less than thirteen New York politicians. He covered his tracks pretty well, habitually with Democrats but sporadically with Republicans like Pataki. For Weinstein and Pataki, campaign contributions had helped foster friendship. Weinstein helped boost Pataki's daughter, Allison's career, as she was an historical novelist. A year before Pataki's call, Weinstein hosted a book party for her. Before that, when her husband suffered a stroke, Weinstein helped secure the right experts.

Weinstein had kept up his calls to Boies about the NBC problem. Following his conversation with Lack, he'd sustained reaching out to NBC executives, and had assuredly reported to people around him that the story was dead. However, it wasn't long before he called Boies back, sounding less certain. He sounded angry, saying he was going to get to the bottom of this. After the call with Pataki, Weinstein placed new sets of calls to Phil Griffin, Andy Lack, and Noah Oppenheim. So often had he shouted these names that the assistants had begun to call them the triumvirate. By August that year, Weinstein was increasingly turning to Oppenheim. Nevertheless Griffin, whom Weinstein told his that staff he knew best, had been an entity of initial and concentrated focus, and continued to be a pillar.

CHAPTER 27: ALTAR

KEY TAKEAWAYS

- Greenberg said that legal had retained the edited version of the script

Initially, the news from the executive suites of NBC Universal seemed good. Greenberg called to explain that legal had retained the edited version of the script. And from an editorial angle, he added that everything in there was reportable. I then said that we seek comment, and go into edit. But he responded saying that being reportable doesn't mean it airs, and that at that point, it goes to Noah and Andy.

I resisted, saying that if legal approved, and he also considered it reportable, why did we have to go through them? He muttered something about their decisions being above his pay grade. He opined that they may have questions that have nothing to do with what's reportable or not, or merely concerned about whether it's good for TV. Greenberg continued, saying that I had an implausible print piece.

Later, McHugh and I sat in a conference room, baffled over the comment. Finally, he spoke, saying I might save the story by taking it to somewhere else. I turned to him to be sure he was aware of the implications of what he just said. We had worked so hard on this, and McHugh had produced the hell out of the story, as a television piece. We'd shot, by this point, eight on-camera interviews. All of that would be a waste in the setup Greenberg had casually proposed. And if I wanted to take it elsewhere, the possibilities were slim, for the footage was owned by NBC Universal and, in turn, the Comcast Corporation. Voicing out, I said we were running this here and produced by you. McHugh replied, "Okay," sounding less certain.

CHAPTER 28: PAVONINE

KEY TAKEAWAYS

- Oppenheim mentioned said that we had some anonymous sourcing.

In all of my years at 30 Rock, the third-floor waiting area often cycled through several arrangements of furniture. That August, there was a low chair and a little table with a fan of the kind of months-old magazines that tend to ornament waiting rooms, I approached Oppenheim's assistant, Anna, to have a little chit-chat. She mentioned that she guessed we guys are working on something big, giving me a wide smile. I walked into Oppenheim's office. He made no attempt to rise or move to the couch. He appeared nervous. I asked where he had his head. Oppenheim shifted in his seat, after which he said that we have some anonymous sourcing in here. I told him that we were leading with a woman we name, showing her face and hearing her voice. I was referring to Gutierrez.

He raised concerns about her credibility, saying that Weinstein's lawyers could say, they're in a public place, nothing actually happens. I then mentioned that Weinstein had admitted to something having happened before, something serious and specific. Again, he came at me saying Weinstein was only trying to get rid of her. I turned to him, telling him that we had sources on the force and in the DA's office, saying she was credible. I suggested that we disclose all of that, and allow the public listen and decide. Once more, he shook his head, and looked at the page again.

CHAPTER 29: FAKAKTA

KEY TAKEAWAYS

- I left for New York magazine.

Oppenheim had just said to me 'go with God'. And of all places to go to, I was headed to New York magazine. My interviews were all locked up on NBC's servers. Motioning to McHugh, I told him what had just happened with Oppenheim. "McHugh was upset, convinced that they were trying to get us to wrap up our reporting. I looked at him and nodded. This was the end.

Back at our compartments, McHugh glanced around, and opened a desk drawer. He produced a silver rectangle, whilst telling me that I did have the interviews. He slid across the desk a USB hard drive, with "Poison Valley" written in black Sharpie on one corner. I was hesitant, but he insisted. He called it backup, and I laughed. I told him he was going to be fired, but we both had to face this- neither of us was going to have a job after this.

I moved in like I wanted to hug him. He simply waved me off, and said that I shouldn't allow them bury this. A few minutes afterwards, I headed for the safe-deposit box at the bank, walking quickly, not wanting to give Oppenheim the chance to reconsider his suggestion that I take the story somewhere else. But I didn't know whom to call. I looked at my phone and saw Auletta's email from the previous day. If there was an outlet that knew the challenges of going up against Weinstein, it was The New Yorker. I dialed Auletta.

He was shocked to find out they were not running it despite all that I had. He told me he'd make some calls and get back to me. I'd been trying to reach Jonathan since after the meeting with Oppenheim. I texted him, telling him to call me, after which I began to pour my anger out, telling him just how much I needed him, and he was nowhere to be found. When he finally called, he was annoyed. I told him I was just dealing with a lot, and felt like I was alone; to which he replied that I wasn't. So, I asked him to come be with me. He responded saying that I was aware that he couldn't do that. By the time I got off the call, I was descending into the subterranean vault. I put the hard drive in the deposit box and watched as it slid back into place with a nails-on-chalkboard squeal.

CHAPTER 30: BOTTLE

KEY TAKEAWAYS

- Corvo had dealt with tough stories about sexual assault allegations

The day after I met with Oppenheim, private investigators had a field day just outside my door. Khaykin was already there when Ostrovskiy strolled over from the bagel place around the corner. Ostrovskiy had texted to find out if Khaykin wanted anything. Few minutes afterwards, they took their positions on the street outside, watching.

After my meeting with Oppenheim, I sent an email to David Corvo, and we had an agreement to meet. I got into my apartment, put on a white button-down shirt, shoved my notes into a bag, and headed out. It was just a bit past eight thirty when the private investigators noted a young man with fair hair, decked in a white shirt with a knapsack. They studied the character. Of course, they had been given reference photos of me, and had also undertaken additional database searches. A bunch of surveillance business was guesswork, but this looked like their spot. Ostrovskiy drove, recording on a Panasonic camcorder. Khaykin chased on foot, descending into the Columbus Circle subway stop, and then getting on a downtown train. For private investigators, long days of surveillance was the same as few opportunities for bathroom breaks.

By the time I made it to Rockefeller Plaza, I'd perspired through the white shirt. Corvo smiled and asked how my work was going, mentioning that he heard we were going to be working together. I ran Corvo through the basics: the audio, the numerous allegations against Harvey Weinstein that had remained in the script after the legal review, Gutierrez's unwavering willingness to be named and to lead the story, and so on. He nodded gently, after which he said it did sound compelling. This was the deal. Corvo had dealt with tough stories about sexual assault allegations before. In 1999, throughout Andy Lack's previous tenure at NBC News, Corvo had supervised the network's interview with Juanita Broaddrick, who had accused Bill Clinton of rape twenty-one years earlier. The network had revised the interview for quite a while after it was recorded, and aired it only after Broaddrick was frustrated and had taken the story to the Wall Street Journal, the Washington Post, and the New York Times.

CHAPTER 31: SYZYGY

KEY TAKEAWAYS

- Weinstein was getting irritated by a lack of information.

Harvey Weinstein was getting irritated by a lack of information. Boies placed a call across to Lack like he promised Weinstein. He asked Lack if work on the story was continuing. Lack was realistic and earnest, remaining quiet for the greater part of the call; the same way he was during the earlier conversation with Weinstein in which the studio head had opined that sleeping with employees was common practice.

When Lack was the executive producer of West 57th in the late eighties, he had pursued sexual relationships with underlings and talent, despite being married at the time. According to Jane Wallace, one of the show's correspondents then, Lack was relentless. She said when she started work at the show, Lack asked her to dinner with him on a daily basis for almost a month, in the name of wanting to celebrate her contract. She asked what I would have done if I were in her shoes, knowing fully well that a refusal to celebrate with him spelt trouble. Wallace admitted that it was in the end, consensual, but that beyond getting flirted with, she got worked over.

Eventually, the relationship went sour and Lack became unpredictable. And upon leaving the show, he yelled at her saying she would never get credit. Subtly, the network played a fast one on her, offering her a substantial payout to sign a binding nondisclosure agreement. She accepted. And it wasn't until she got out of there that she knew the weight of what she had done. She said that if Lack had not been that way, she would have kept the job. As a matter of fact, she loved the job.

As I flew to LA the evening after the meeting at The New Yorker, Greenberg called McHugh, sounding panicky. He said Oppenheim had told him to pause this. I asked if this meant that I couldn't report anything else. He said that Greenberg replied that this was a direct order from our boss.

The following morning, Greenberg called me and said the same thing- We can't shoot this interview. We are pausing. To be clear, I asked if Greenberg was y ordering me to cancel this interview, but he simply said that it was a pause. "I then asked how how long this pause was for and the exact reason why NBC News was ordering us to stop reporting. He finally responded saying that Harvey's lawyers have made the argument that every employee is subject to a nondisclosure agreement, and that we couldn't just go cheering them to breach those.

CHAPTER 32: HURRICANE

KEY TAKEAWAYS

- Emily Nestor agrees.

Emily Nestor and I sat down to have some coffee at a coffee shop in Brentwood. At the same time, scenes of destruction flashed on a television in the corner. Since Nestor said that she was open to revealing her face if NBC wanted it, she hadn't demonstrated any signs of backing down. But I also failed to tell her that the story's official support had degenerated, and that going on the record now meant a print fact-checking process. I told her that I was going to send my draft to The New Yorker, and that the magazine would decide whether or not to take on the story based on the draft. She told me she had spent a lot of time thinking about this, and then she said she was going to do it.

I ran out of the coffee shop to complete the draft. The reporting was described thus- The New Yorker would be in view of that which NBC News had sent away: In the passage of a nine-month examination, five women told me directly that Harvey Weinstein committed multiple acts of sexual harassment and abuse. The accusations range from inappropriate sexual intentions directed at employees, to groping and touching of the kind confessed to in the NYPD tape, to two claims of rape. The allegations span close to twenty years. Many of the women worked for Weinstein, and all of their claims involved apparently professional meetings, which they claim Weinstein used to lure them to hotels where they experienced unwanted sexual advances. In not less than three cases, Weinstein employed the use of large financial clearances with strict nondisclosure agreements to prevent criminal proceedings and public revelation. Sixteen past and present administrators and assistants at Weinstein's companies substantiated those claims, saying they saw unwanted sexual advances, inappropriate touching, and a pattern that included Weinstein using company resources to set up sexual liaisons of the type described in the allegations. I sent the draft to Foley-Mendelssohn. On a muted TV in Jonathan's living room, Hurricane Harvey did havoc.

CHAPTER 33: GOOSE

KEY TAKEAWAYS

- Weinstein had become apprehensive

By this time, Weinstein had become apprehensive, instilling his usual blend of fear and influence in the media. David Pecker of American Media Inc., had long been a close friend. All of a sudden however, he began to show up more frequently in Weinstein's emails. At some point, Weinstein proposed a union to buy Rolling Stone magazine for Pecker to add to his media empire, and run from behind. At first, Pecker objected, and then agreed.

Weinstein augmented his outreach to NBC as well. There were tons of emails and calls to Deborah Turness, Oppenheim's precursor, who was now in control of global content. Weinstein planned cutting a deal with Turness around a documentary he was making about Clinton. Turness wrote back, saying that the Hillary doc series sounds undeniably striking and that she pledged to turn the platforms into dedicated Hillary channels for several nights. Weinstein also mailed Ron Meyer, the veteran head of Universal Studios and vice chairman of NBC Universal, saying he wanted to talk to him about Universal doing his home video and VOD. Meyer responded that he would love to make this work. Soon after, Meyer wrote that he looked forward to their being in business together. The deal never went ahead. Weinstein had appeared reassured after Lanny Davis's report back on the meeting with Oppenheim and Boies's update after the call with Lack. Weinstein had taken both as clear-cut validation that the story was dropped, and perhaps, me with it. But he wanted more. He placed another round of calls from his legal team to NBC's, and it wasn't long before Susan Weiner was on the phone with one of Davis's attorneys, saying I was no longer working for NBC News.

CHAPTER 34: LETTER

KEY TAKEAWAYS

- Weinstein had been bullying everyone linked to me.

All through the month of September, my representatives at CAA had been calling. Alan Berger, my agent, Bryan Lourd, his boss and one of the heads of the agency, all called saying Weinstein had been bullying them. I told them that if I had a story about Weinstein in the near future, I would meet with him, as early as was fitting. When Lourd delivered the message to him, he refused to take no for an answer. Instead, Weinstein showed up at the agent's office in Los Angeles and ranted for more than an hour. He said he was far from perfect and has been working on himself for a very long time now. Worse still, he felt like he was being painted with an old brush.

I thought to myself that I did not sign up for this. Weinstein said he'd hired a lot of lawyers so as not to create problems for me and that a meeting had to ensue, immediately. The next Tuesday, there was another email from Weinstein to Lourd demanding to talk immediately, and an update from Lourd in response. Throughout Friday, Weinstein kept ringing

Berger and Lourd. He told Berger his legal team was ready. Specifically, he mentioned Harder, and Boies and Lisa Bloom. A few hours later, copies of a letter began arriving at various offices at CAA. I thought of the scene from Harry Potter where invitations to attend Hogwarts start flying in through the fireplace and the letterbox and the windows. Berger called to read me the letter- Charles Harder sending Harvey Weinstein's threat to sue me, based on an arrangement he suggested had been reached with NBC News.

Pages of demands that I preserve documents in anticipation of potential litigation followed after. NBC later denied ever reaching an agreement with Weinstein and said Harder was misrepresenting their communications. I forwarded the letter to Bertoni, who said he didn't want to disregard it, but that it did strikes him as silly.

CHAPTER 35: MIMIC

KEY TAKEAWAYS

- I didn't assent to Harder's threat

I didn't assent to Harder's threat. As a matter of fact, I did not even respond to it. I just kept reporting. That month, I got Mira Sorvino on the phone. Sorvino, the daughter of actor, Paul Sorvino, was a prominent figure in the nineties. She'd won an Oscar, in 1995, for Mighty Aphrodite—one of Woody Allen's films which Weinstein had dispersed and had stressed in his threats to NBC. And she'd been a bona fide movie star for a year or two after, resulting in a leading role in another Weinstein film, Mimic. After that, she simply vanished.

In our first call, Sorvino sounded terrified. She said she had already lost so much of her career to this form of sexual harassment from Weinstein while they were at work, together. In September 1995, she found herself in a hotel room with Weinstein. He was making attempts to kiss her when she ran away, creating ways to tell him off. Then, she left the room. A few weeks later, in New York City, her phone rang after midnight. It was Weinstein asking to get together. Sorvino offered to meet him at an all-night diner, but he said he was coming over to her apartment and hung up. She told Weinstein that her new boyfriend was on his way, he seemed unhappy and left. Sorvino said that she felt afraid and intimidated; and when she told a female employee at Miramax about the harassment, the woman's reaction "was shock and horror that I had mentioned it. Sorvino was convinced that, after she rejected Weinstein, he'd reacted against her, blacklisted her, hurt her career. But she acknowledged the difficulty of ever proving this point.

CHAPTER 36: HUNTER

KEY TAKEAWAYS

- Asia Argento, the Italian actress had a Weinstein story to tell

For quite some time, a number of sources had come forward to tell me that Asia Argento, the Italian actress had a Weinstein story to tell. Her father was quite famous for his horror films. She once played a huge role as a glamorous thief in "B. Monkey," a crime drama distributed by Weinstein, and was quickly sized up by Hollywood as a stock exotic femme fatale type, a role she gamely played in the Vin Diesel vehicle "XXX." This however proved that something was amiss, a hint that there was something dark, and perhaps damaged about her.

Like many others, she as no longer in touch with her agents and managers. I had followed her on social media and we had liked one another's photos. Soon after, we spoke over the phone. She was scared. In my interviews with her, she would tell me that Weinstein assaulted her when they worked together. Sometime in 1997, she was invited to a party thrown by Miramax. She was invited by Lombardo, the head of Miramax

Italy. However, instead of leading her to the party, Lombardo had led her to Weinstein's hotel room. Weinstein began by praising her work, after which he left the room. He retuned wearing a bathrobe and holding a bottle of lotion in hand, asking me to give him a massage. She told him straight up that she wasn't a fool.

Reluctantly, she agreed to give him a massage, after which he pulled her skirt up, forced her legs wide apart and had sex with her, orally, despite repeatedly telling him to stop. Sadly, she was beaten by the guilt that she did not fight him off physically. Worse still, she felt responsible.

He kept contacting her, seeming as though he was obsessed with her and offering to get her expensive gifts. The story however was complicated in that not only did Argento allow him have his way, but she gave in to his advances over time. she confessed to having occasional sexual encounters with him in the years that followed, because she felt she had to, for fear that Weinstein would ruin her career if she did not comply.

Years later, she became a single mother dealing with childcare, and Weinstein again offered to pay for the services of a nanny, while she felt indebted to him, and submitted to his sexual advances.

CHAPTER 37: HEIST

KEY TAKEAWAYS

- Some of the accusers refused to talk at all

Nearly every day, I would encounter a road block. Some of the accusers refused to talk at all. All summer, I'd gone after Lauren O'Connor, a former literary scout at the Weinstein Company who had written an internal memo complaining about Weinstein's behavior with employees in 2015. Weinstein had been verbally abusive to her, and she'd learned of his predation. At one point, a young lady had banged on the door of her hotel room, visibly shaken and crying, and finally telling a familiar story about Weinstein propositioning her for a massage.

In the memo, O'Connor wrote that she was a twenty-eight-year-old woman trying to make a living. She described Harvey Weinstein as a 64-year-old, world famous man, stating that this was his company. But like many others, O'Connor had signed a nondisclosure agreement and was still too afraid to talk. Late that September, an in-between called to say that O'Connor had consulted a lawyer and made her final decision-she will not engage, with anyone at all. O'Connor didn't want me using her name. This was a huge blow to me, as I had her name from documents. But the in-between had described her panic. Painfully, I became more aware that I was a man writing a story about women's consent, confronting a woman saying she didn't want her life upended in this way. Eventually, she would begin to tell her story publicly. But at the time, I promised I wouldn't include her. Then there were those who hesitated. The actress Claire Forlani would later post an open letter on social media about her struggle over whether to describe to me her claim that Weinstein had harassed her.

CHAPTER 38: CELEBRITY

KEY TAKEAWAYS

- Throughout the whole of September, the New Yorker work gained great stride and force

Throughout the whole of September, the New Yorker work gained great stride and force. The whole team examined the reports which kept accumulation, and kept poring over the drafts. I often stayed late at the World Trade center, where I made reporting calls. On a particular day, I arrived home to find a silver Nissan pathfinder parked outside my house. I jolted, recognizing the vehicle. And while I still had no proof as to whether I was being followed or not, a suspicion lay awake within me.

A number of my friends had offered to have me over for summer. I kept telling them that I was fine. But one of my friends, Sophie had said she was used to security threats and told me to take my suspicions seriously. And that if I needed somewhere to stay, I should put a call across to her. I finally did just that.

At the end of the month, I packed up my belongings and moved into a section of a building where Sophie's family owned lots of floors. There were layers of security to this place, and I did feel much safer here.

However, it was still increasingly difficult to shake off the paranoia that I was being watched.

There were also indications that the New York Times was closing in on the story. I had recently learned that two different investigative reporters were at the forefront of the paper's efforts, chasing sources just as I had.

CHAPTER 39: FALLOUT

KEY TAKEAWAYS

- Weinstein began with his threats

I had my sources as well as Weinstein's intermediaries spread around the globe. My phone rang in never ending style. I hardly got the chance to sleep. I looked pale and much thinner than I had when summer began.

When the fact-checkers began to call sources far and wide, Weinstein began with his threats. The first Monday of October had him send a legal letter to the New Yorker through Harder. The letter stated that the reporting was defamatory, and demanded that we refrained from publishing the story. Quickly, he brought in all sorts of statements about the TWC and the NBC, particularly stating that I was working for the NBC and that the NBC rejected the story and terminated the project.

Apparently, the letter was informed by Weinstein's recent conversation with Woody Allen. According to the letter, my sister's sexual assault had disqualified me from reporting on Weinstein, narrowing my reports down to personal feelings and misplaced anger.

According to him, I was brainwashed into finding my sisters claim true.

One thing that struck me was how the arguments that the letter presented were so similar to those that Oppenheim had reeled out to me. Bloom also came to mind as she swore to defend my sister, and I was appalled to realize just how much people would sell their souls doe Harvey Weinstein.

CHAPTER 40: DINOSAUR

KEY TAKEAWAYS

- Things were really changing for Harvey Weinstein

That October, things were really changing for Harvey Weinstein. He had become haggard looking. He was often thrown into fits of rage, but this time around, his outbursts were worse than the usual. He grew suspicious inside his own company. And on the 3rd of October, he hired an IT specialist to locate and delete a file which was tilted 'HW Friends'- a file that mapped out locations and contact information of tons of women, the world around.

On the 5th of October, Weinstein summoned his defense team to his offices on Greenwich Street, where an improvised war room was situated in a green room. Gathered there were Bloom, Howard, Pam Lubell and Denise Doyle Chambers. Davis and Harder called in, with the assistant placing them on speaker. Weinstein was losing his mind as he shouted at the top of his lungs. The Times story was yet to be published, but he had been told it was in the offing. Name after name, he roared at everyone present, thinking up who he hoped would defend him when the stories began to break.

Downtown, I took a seat at a vacant desk at the New Yorker, and called the Weinstein Company for comment. The front desk assistant who picked up said he'd check if Weinstein was available. Soon, I heard his voice over the phone, mockery filling his every sentence. He asked to know why I was calling, and I simply told him that in a bid to be fair, I'd include anything he had to say. I also asked if he was comfortable with my recording. He seemed to panic, and dropped the phone. Later in the afternoon, the same thing happened. I finally got around to talking to him later, where I asked series of questions. He didn't respond to them, but rather, told me to send all my questions to Lisa Bloom.

CHAPTER 41: MEAN

KEY TAKEAWAYS

- Weinstein told his staff they were going to war.

Weinstein declared his relief at the Times story, and its timing, and went on to issue a supposedly stimulating message to his staff, by telling them they were going to war. There and then, an assistant quit, and left. Weinstein asked that he stop, and receive a glowing recommendation from him. Unbelievable!

Same day, later in the evening, the board of Directors of the Weinstein Company gathered for an emergency conference call. All nine members of the board would be on the line, Weinstein inclusive. For a number of years now, a small group of directors had sought to oust Weinstein, while a majority of loyalists considered him vital to the success of the company. Painful as it may sound, stories of abuse by powerful people are also stories of a failure of board culture. Both Weinstein and his brother, Bob, had two seats on the board, while the company's charter allowed for them to name a third person. Subtly, Weinstein was able to install loyalists in most of the remaining seats, thereby controlling a whooping six out of nine board seats. Weinstein used this means to evade being accountable. And in the case that a board member, Lance Maerov, whom he considered an adversary, demanded to see his personal files, Weinstein and Boies would succeed in preventing this from happening, and would rather hire an attorney from the outside to render a hazy summary of its contents.

On this occasion, Weinstein got on the phone with the remaining members of the board, denying every allegation and arguing that the Times story would blow over. The call degenerated into a bitter outburst from both factions, and between the Weinstein brothers. Lubell for one continued to say that they were going to open up the books on Weinstein.

CHAPTER 42: EDIFY

KEY TAKEAWAYS

- An additional source joined our story

After our story was published by the Times, an additional source joined our story. There was an allegation by Lucia Evans, a marketing consultant. In 2004, Weinstein approached Evans at a club in Manhattan. Evans was just about to start her senior year at Middlebury College, and was trying to break into the world of acting. Weinstein got her cell number, and soon enough, he began calling late at night, or having his assistant call her and asking to meet. She refused the late night advances, but agreed to meet with a casting executive during the day.

Upon arriving for the meeting, the building was filled with people. She was taken into an office with exercise equipment. Weinstein was there all by himself. He began by flattering her after which he assaulted her and forced her to perform oral sex on him.

October 10, the final edit of the story was put together. When it was done, I wandered over to one of the office's windows and looked out at the Hudson with a numb feeling. My phone continued to chime all day long, with messages arriving in never ending style.

CHAPTER 43: CABAL

KEY TAKEAWAYS

- Oppenheim said they'd give me an NBC title again.

Noah Oppenheim texted me the next day, sounding very confident that we both could get a new deal done. Less than an hour after the story ran his call came through. He continually expressed how glad he was that it all worked out in the end, explaining just how much people were calling and asking for means to reach me. Some even went as far as wanting to book me to talk about the article. For the appearances, Oppenheim said they'd give me an NBC title again.

I told Oppenheim that the only reason I was hesitant about going on NBC was because it would make e put him and anyone there in a very awkward position. Frankly, I told him that I did not want to be in a position where I would have to hide anything at all.

Both Oppenheim and Kornblau made the issue much more difficult to avoid. And at this point, several media reporters had called me, stating that both executives had dissembled as regards the history of the story in their background conversations. I was stressed out, and directed all my calls to Raabe, the New Yorker's head of communications.

Oppenheim asked if I would get over to 30 Rock quickly to shoot a spot for Nightly News. Truthfully, I felt I was being used to salvage a PR problem. But the women's claims deserved all the exposure on NBC's platforms. And honestly, I wanted my job back!

The next ring my phone had was a congratulatory one from Matt Lauer!

CHAPTER 44: CHARGER

KEY TAKEAWAYS

- Oppenheim said we had to release a statement saying that NBC never had the story.

Maddow got her call the moment she was off air. With her phone pressed to her ear, she paced up and down the set. Oppenheim's call came through next. He sounded nervous. He said that he was being told we had to release a statement saying more forcefully, on the record, that NBC never had the story, and wanted me to sign on to it.

We wasted no time getting back to the circular arguments from his office, although he had suddenly gone from making the case for why the story shouldn't run to actually arguing that he hadn't made that case initially. I asked if he ever spoke to Weinstein, which he denied. I then reminded him that when he presented me with the article about Harvey working with Woody Allen, he particularly used the phrase- Harvey says. At this point, he began to groan and wail and blurted out saying Weinstein called him once and that the call stretched on for hours. Kornblau had conferenced in and pressed him to sign a compromise statement that conceded the story had passed a legal and standards review, but also failed to meet our standards.

At the time, I knew none of this. I was simply trying to salvage my future with the executives. I told them I was not, and could not join a false statement, but that I would avoid answering further questions like Maddow's.

CHAPTER 45: NIGHTGOWN

KEY TAKEAWAYS

- The women involved in the stories were reacting

The women involved in the stories were reacting as well. While some ere pained, others were excited that the truth was now made public. Each and every one of them described a weight having been lifted off their shoulders. McGowan particularly thanked me with a beautiful note.

The day the story broke, Annabella Sciorra sent word saying that I did an amazing job of not only outing him, but carrying the pain of all those women along. I called her back, and it was the she managed to tell me her story. And like the others, she had struggled to speak about Weinstein for over twenty years, after he violently raped her, and harassed her sexually over the next couple of years.

CHAPTER 46: PRETEXTING

KEY TAKEAWAYS

- I followed up on Freedman's call

Seth Freedman was a London stockbroker who moved to Israel and served in a combat unit in the Israeli Defense Forces for fifteen months, before he turned whistle blower who took to the pages of the Guardian to expose his financial firm's manipulation of wholesale gas prices, for which he was fired. He was smallish in stature, and he cut a beautiful profile.

In October 2017, after meeting with Sciorra, I followed up on Freedman's call saying I wanted to talk. He responded beautifully to my WhatsApp messages, explaining that he had been working with an English paper to get some of the stories out. He later explained how he passed recordings he had made of his conversations with McGowan and another accuser of Weinstein's to the Guardian's Sunday publication, the Observer and how articles were published based on he interviews. These articles were devoid of Freedman being mentioned.

CHAPTER 47: RUNNING

KEY TAKEAWAYS

- I received a complete record of all of Black Cube's work for Weinstein.

A mail was sent, encrypted from Proton Mail, bearing the name 'sleeper 1973'. Attached to it was a complete record of all of Black Cube's work for Weinstein. It was detailed, from the very first contract signed October 28, 2016 to the many others that followed after. The last arrangement promised services through November. Black Cube promised a number of things among which were a dedicated team of expert intelligence officers in the USA and any other necessary country, a full time agent who will be based in New York and Los Angeles and who would be available full time to assist the client and his attorneys for the next four months.

And then there were invoices- eye popping fees that totaled over a million dollars. All of the contracts were signed by Yanus, the Black Cube Director. Boies's law firm represented the New York Times. But there lay the esteemed lawyer's signature on a contract to kill the paper's reporting and obtain Mc Gowan's book.

CHAPTER 48: GAS LIGHT

KEY TAKEAWAYS

- Sleeper refused to meet in person

Rohde and every other person at the New Yorkers pressed that I had to find out who Sleeper 1973 was. I dismissed it saying it was possibly a Woody Allen reference. But whoever sleeper was, he refused to meet in person. He insisted that even online methods were capable of being monitored, and that he didn't want anything that would come back to him. Despite all my pleas, he kept sending messages from the encrypted email address. Unable to identify who Anna the undercover detective was, I asked Sleeper for any leads he might have. He responded saying that Anna's real name was Stella Pen, and that she already had 125 pictures of Rose's book. He attached three pictures to the mail which I immediately sent to McGowan and Ben Wallace. They both remembered who she was instantly. Diana Flip!

CHAPTER 49: VACUUM

KEY TAKEAWAYS

- Over the years, Kroll had helped Weinstein thwart reporters

It was beyond Black Cube. One call led to more calls, and into the underworld, divulging all the secrets of private intelligence. Objectors kept feeding me with information about their intelligence agencies, with leaders leaking about their competitors with the sole aim of broadening the focus of my reporting beyond their own activities.

Several documents lit up Weinstein's long relationship with Kroll and Dan Karson. Over the years, Kroll had helped Weinstein thwart reporters. In 2016 and 2017, they had both worked closely with Weinstein again. In an email sent in October 2016, Karson sent Weinstein eleven images of McGowan and Weinstein together at events in the years after he sexually assaulted her. This they called the money shot. And as Wallace worked on the story, Kroll continued his search for damaging information about him and his editor at New York magazine, Adam Moss.

CHAPTER 50: PLAYMATE

KEY TAKEAWAYS

- It wasn't only Weinstein that the tabloid empire had worked with to suppress stories.
- At the heart of the mystery was a woman named Karen McDougal

A vein was opened up with the reporting on Dylan Howard and the Enquirer. One after the other, sources within and outside American Media Inc. called, saying that it wasn't only Weinstein that the tabloid empire had worked with to suppress stories.

Later that November, I got a letter from a lawyer named Carol Heller. She explained to me that a report that the wall street journal had published in the fall of 2016 about a playboy model who'd signed over to AMI the exclusive rights to her story about a purported affair with Donald Trump- a story AMI never published.

She mentioned that the woman at the heart of the mystery was named Karen McDougal and that she was still too scared to open up. She said that if I could get her and others around the transaction to open up, I might be able to reveal how the contract with AMI came to be, and how the culture of nondisclosure agreements and buried stories existed beyond Hollywood, but into politics as well.

CHAPTER 51: CHUPACABRA

KEY TAKEAWAYS

- McDougal's contract was part of a pattern of AMI working to suppress stories for Trump

As at the time we published, I had gotten wind of another transaction which might bring to bear the fact that the McDougal's contract was part of a pattern of AMI working to suppress stories for Trump. Dylan Howard's friends and colleagues had contacted me saying that he had boasted that he had evidence that Trump may have fathered a child with his former housekeeper in the late 1980s. Howard said a lot of things when he was drunk, or high, including telling me they would pay for stories and nit publish, so as to protect people, one of his friends had said.

There was no evidence that the rumor about the love child was true. But that spring, a lot of fingers pointed towards AMI actually buying rights to the dubious claim, after which it worked to prevent it from being disclosed.

CHAPTER 52: CIRCLE

KEY TAKEAWAYS

- Howard had a mean streak, and not less than ten people said the same thing.

Howard had a mean streak, and not less than ten people who had worked with him told me the same thing. It was later learned that he openly described his sexual partners in the newsroom, freely discussed the sex lives of female employees and even forced women to watch or listen to pornographic content. Because of complaints from female colleagues, AMI had to launch and internal inquiry in 2012. This was led by an outside consultant, and the report maintained that the company found no serious wrongdoing. The general counsel admitted that women had lodged complaints about Howard, but he later denied all of the allegations, of misconduct, leaving the women disgruntled.

CHAPTER 53: AXIOM

KEY TAKEAWAYS

- Black Cube's activities

After the love child story, I stumbled on my first set of clues about the Black Cube's activities after the Weinstein job. A call came in, with the Caller ID reading "Axiom". A few moments later, a text came through. Whoever sent the text message said he was trying to reach me directly and privately, about a Frypan that's scratch resistant. Prior to that time, I had posted a picture of a frying pan marketed under the label "Black Cube" "Scratch Resistant…"

As the car slipped into a tunnel, I sent a text back, requesting that the person says more about who he was. He responded saying he did surveillance, and later said that we would need to meet discreetly and make sure we are not followed.

CHAPTER 54: PEGASUS

KEY TAKEAWAYS

- InfoTactic and Black Cube.

Initially, Ostrovskiy did not want to divulge his boss' name. But the clues were already there. In one of the images he had shown me, the plates of the Nissan vehicle were very visible. I typed in the name I came up with, and pulled up a promotional video with a Russian man named Roman Khaykin- founder of InfoTactic Group. Khaykin was very serious about his skills which ranged from phone tracking to his ability to illegally obtain financial records.

Ostrovskiy kept sharing insights about InfoTactic's ongoing operations for Black Cube. Sometimes, I would go to the appointed location myself. At other times, I would send colleagues who were less likely to be spotted. Just as it was with Weinstein, the Black Cube pattern remained the same as undercover Black Cube agents repeatedly met with cybercrime and technology experts in luxe hotels.

CHAPTER 55: MELTING

KEY TAKEAWAYS

- Matt Lauer is fired overnight.

The year after the Weinstein story was troubled at NBC news, Savannah Guthrie announced that Matt Lauer had been fired overnight for inappropriate sexual behavior in the workplace. She was heartbroken as she called Lauer her dear friend and emphasized that he was loved by many people there.

The management was shocked about Lauer. Apparently, this unnamed colleague had lodged the first complaint in the over twenty years he had spent working at the NBC. Following the announcement, Oppenheim gathered members of the investigative unit in the conference room on the fourth floor. He mentioned that while the behavior alleged by this unnamed colleague was unacceptable, the breach lay within the confines of professional and not criminal standards of conduct. Like Lack, Oppenheim also said that the network had been unaware of any complaints about Lauer until two days before, when the colleague came forward. Like many of us, the statement struck most of the journalists present as strange.

After a series of investigations, it was discovered that Lauer actually had several women complaining about his behavior, but had somehow managed to be swept under the carpet for years. Finally, all the allegations had come forward.

CHAPTER 56: ZDOROVIE

The complaint that resulted in Lauer being fried ended pretty much the same way- a payout and a non-disclosure agreement. When Brooke Nevils, the lady in question and I spoke for the first time, she completely doubted if she would ever be able to go public. She confessed to living in terror all her life.

In the course of the past two years, she had attempted suicide, hospitalized for post-traumatic stress disorder, descended into heavy drinking, lost weight and visited the doctor countless numbers of times. She said she had lost everything she cared about.

Since she was thirteen, she wanted to be a journalist. Lauer raped her, robbing her of her dream.

CHAPTER 57: SPIKE

KEY TAKEAWAYS

- More men get fired

Lauer wasn't the only one affected. Since the Weinstein story became public, the NBC was bugged with all sorts of allegations about its men. Shortly after the story on Weinstein, NBC fired Mark Halperin, the station's most prominent political analyst, after several reports reached CNN from women who said he had been harassing and assaulting women in the workplace, by grabbing, exposing himself and even rubbing an erection against one woman.

Shortly after, Matt Zimmerman was also fired for similar allegations. More followed. Tom Brokaw was also accused of unwanted advances. Brokaw's position particularly hit me because he once sent me an email where he called the killing of the Weinstein story by the NBC a self- inflicted wound. How then was it possible that a principled defender of a tough story was also a part of the system that made women unsafe and uncomfortable, leaving no room for accountability?

Too many names continued to emerge and supposed secrets, exposed. Women were speaking up, and identifying their abusers, publicly.

CHAPTER 58: LAUNDER

KEY TAKEAWAYS

- McHugh resigned!

Because McHugh refused to yield to the network president's characterizations of the reporting, Oppenheim grew agitated and cursed at him. He spent the entire year grappling with fallout from the story as well. He continued to speak up in group meetings; he once mentioned that no one knew his name, and that they were free to say whatever they wanted about him. I simply told him to do what was best for his girls.

Finally, McHugh decided he couldn't take the money. A year after he was ordered to stand down from on the Weinstein reporting, he resigned, he then gave an interview to the New York Times where he said that the reporting had been killed at the very highest levels of the NBC, that he was ordered to stop taking calls about the story, and that the network had lied about what truly happened.

CHAPTER 59: BLACKLIST

Following the first New Yorker story, I was faced with a dilemma similar to McHugh's. For a while, I kept my promise to dodge questions about the story's history at NBC. Journalists like Stephen Colbert of CBS found it strange that I responded saying I didn't want the story to be about me, and so I changed the subject. At the height of the evasive interviews, my sister called, and said to me that I was covering for them. I told her I wasn't lying. She replied, saying I was omitting, which was equally dishonest. Immediately, I remembered the low points between us both, and how I had told her to shut up about her own allegation.

If there was something I had learnt, it was that in the end, the courage of women cannot be stamped out, and stores, the true, big stories may be caught, but the can never be killed.

Made in the USA
San Bernardino, CA
16 December 2019

61601099R00083